M000216737

The
Essential
Wisdom
of the Irish

The
Essential
Wisdom
of the Irish

edited by
Carol Kelly-Gangi

FALL RIVER PRESS

New York

In loving memory of my grandparents
Marie and Tom Kelly
Ann and Joe Lynch

FALL RIVER PRESS

New York

An Imprint of Sterling Publishing
387 Park Avenue South
New York, NY 10016

ISBN 978-1-4351-3761-5 (print format)
ISBN 978-1-4351-3910-7 (ebook)

Distributed in Canada by Sterling Publishing
c/o Canadian Manda Group, 165 Dufferin Street
Toronto, Ontario, Canada M6K 3H6
Distributed in the United Kingdom by GMC Distribution Services
Castle Place, 166 High Street, Lewes, East Sussex, England BN7 1XU
Distributed in Australia by Capricorn Link (Australia) Pty. Ltd.
P.O. Box 704, Windsor, NSW 2756, Australia

For information about custom editions, special sales, and premium and corporate
purchases, please contact Sterling Special Sales at 800-805-5489 or specialsales@
sterlingpublishing.com.

Manufactured in the United States of America

2 4 6 8 10 9 7 5 3 1

www.sterlingpublishing.com

Contents

Introduction

What does it mean to be Irish? Writers and scholars through the centuries have offered varying interpretations that touch on such ideas as sharing a kinship with Ireland and her struggles; having a deeply abiding faith (particularly in the Catholic or Protestant traditions); possessing traits such as a self-deprecating sense of humor; having the gift of gab; being a born storyteller, or standing strong in the face of adversity.

In *The Essential Wisdom of the Irish*, hundreds of quotations from and about the Irish people have been gathered together to offer some additional insight into what it means to be Irish. The contributors come from all walks of life and are as diverse as the selections themselves. There are writers and scholars; politicians and journalists; patriots and leaders; artists and entertainers. Though the majority of contributors, of course, hail from Ireland, there is also a grouping of Irish-American contributors interspersed as well. What Irish-Americans have to say about their own version of the Irish experience adds, in my view, a richness that speaks for itself.

The themes that emerge are universal in some respects and singular in others. There is the fierce love of family; the enduring quest for freedom; and the struggle to withstand every form of adversity—including poverty, famine, political oppression, and religious persecution. In the selections that

follow, William Butler Yeats extols the Irish contributions
to literature and political intelligence; George Bernard Shaw
reflects on the stark, physical beauty of the Irish landscape;
Edna O'Brien offers keen insight into the Irish character; and
Oscar Wilde and James Joyce ponder the connection between
life and literature.

In other selections Irish patriots such as Michael Collins,
James Connolly, Eamon de Valera, Robert Emmet, Patrick
Pearse, and Wolfe Tone speak passionately about the cause
for Ireland's freedom. Still other selections reveal the personal
triumphs and struggles that the contributors faced in their
own lives. Daniel O'Connell reflects on his long and happy
marriage; Eamonn McCann describes the chaos in Belfast at
the height of the Troubles; Kerry Kennedy reveals the central
role of the Catholic faith in her family; and Tip O'Neill shares
an invaluable lesson he learned early in his political career.
Rounding out the collection is a sampling of Irish songs,
proverbs, blessings, and a wee bit of Irish humor.

So whether you're looking to reconnect with your own
Irish roots, or are simply interested in learning more about
this ancient people, *The Essential Wisdom of the Irish* is a rich
testament to the men and woman who have embodied the
spirit of endurance, tenacity, and hope through the ages, and
who continue to leave a singular mark on the world in every
field of endeavor.

CAROL KELLY-GANGI
Rumson, New Jersey, 2011

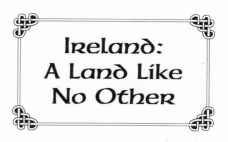

Ireland: A Land Like No Other

Your wits can't thicken in that soft moist air, on those white springy roads, in those misty rushes and brown bogs, on those hillsides of granite rocks and magenta heather. You've no such colours in the sky, no such lure in the distances, no such sadness in the evenings. Oh the dreaming! The dreaming! The torturing, heart scalding, never satisfying dreaming, dreaming, dreaming.

— GEORGE BERNARD SHAW, *John Bull's Other Island,* 1904

O Ireland, isn't it grand you look—
Like a bride in her rich adornin'?
And with all the pent-up love of my heart
I bid you the top o' the mornin'!

—JOHN LOCKE, "The Exile's Return," or
"Morning on the Irish Coast," 1877

Land of Heart's Desire,
Where beauty has no ebb, decay no flood,
But joy is wisdom, Time an endless song.

—WILLIAM BUTLER YEATS, *The Land of Heart's Desire,* 1903

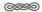

This island is a region of dreams and trifles.

— GEORGE BERKELEY, *The Querist,* 1735

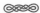

Whenever I dream, it seems I dream
Of Erin's rolling hills—
All its lovely, shimmery lakes
And little babbling rills—
I hear a colleen's lilting laugh
Across a meadow fair
And in my dreams it almost seems
To me that I am there—
O, Ireland! O, Ireland!
We're never far apart
For you and all your beauty
Fill my mind and touch my heart.

—E. GARY BROOKS

In Ireland the inevitable never happens and the unexpected
constantly occurs.

—JOHN PENTLAND MAHAFFY, quoted in *Mahaffy* by
W. B. Stanford and R. B. McDowell, 1971

✧

The graceful Georgian streets and squares, a series of steel
engravings under a wet sky.

—SHANA ALEXANDER, "Dublin Is My Sure Thing,"
LIFE Magazine, September 1966

✧

Dublin with its wide central street, its statues and its time-
darkened buildings, has a dignity such as one associates with
some of the southern towns in the United States—a dignity
of memories and of manners. Its squares, its railed-in areas,
its flights of steps, its tall houses of brick richly-coloured
as wine, give it the air of a splendid relic of the eighteenth
century. It is unforgettably a capital.

—ROBERT LYND, *Home Life in Ireland,* 1909

Dublin, on the east, the Europe-regarding, coast of Ireland, owes her vitality and complexity as a city to a continuous influx of foreign life. The invader, the trader, the opportunist, the social visitor have all added strife or colour.

—ELIZABETH BOWEN, *Collected Impressions,* 1950

Oh, Limerick is beautiful
As everybody knows,
And by that city of my heart
How proud old Shannon flows.

—MICHAEL SCANLON

Irish countrysides are so different from each other that it is not easy to find an interpreting word which will cover them all. Still, there is one thing which gives a unity—a personality, as it were—to Ireland. It is the glory of light which comes towards evening and rests on every field and on every hill and in the street of every town like a strange tide. Everywhere in Ireland, north, south, east, and west, the evening air is, as a fine living poet has perceived, a shimmer as of diamonds.

—ROBERT LYND, *Home Life in Ireland,* 1909

I know a town tormented by the sea
And there time goes slow
That the people see it flow and watch it drowsily.

—MARY DAVENPORT, "Galway"

So I have come into Wicklow, where the fields are sharply green, where a wild beauty hides in the glens, where sudden surprising vistas open up as the road rises and falls; and here I smell for the first time the incense of Ireland, the smoke of turf fires, and here for the first time I see the face of the Irish countryside.

—H. V. MORTON, *In Search of Ireland,* 1930

The power of perpetuating our property in our families is one of the most valuable and interesting circumstances belonging to it, and that which tends the most to the perpetuation of society itself. It makes our weakness subservient to our virtue; it grafts benevolence even upon avarice.

—EDMUND BURKE, *Reflections on the Revolution in France,* 1790

This is a parish in which you understand hunger. But there
are many hungers. There is hunger for food—a natural hunger.
There is the hunger of the flesh—a natural understandable
hunger. There is a hunger for home, for love, for children.
These things are good—they are good because they are
necessary. But there is also the hunger for land. And in this
parish, you, and your fathers before you knew what it was to
starve because you did not own your own land—and that has
increased; this unappeasable hunger for land.

—JOHN B. KEANE, *The Field,* 1966

That Ireland which we dreamed of would be the home of a
people who valued material wealth only as a basis of right
living, of a people who were satisfied with frugal comfort and
devoted their leisure to the things of the spirit; a land whose
countryside would be bright with cosy homesteads, whose
fields and villages would be joyous with sounds of industry,
the romping of sturdy children, the contests of athletic youths,
the laughter of comely maidens; whose firesides would be the
forums of the wisdom of serene old age.

—EAMON DE VALERA, Radio Broadcast, St. Patrick's Day, 1943

Ireland is a peculiar society in the sense that it was a nineteenth century society up to about 1970 and then it almost bypassed the twentieth century.

—JOHN MCGAHERN, Interviewed in *The Observer,* January 2002

Do you not feel that this island is moored only lightly to the sea-bed, and might be off for the Americas at any moment?

—SEBASTIAN BARRY, *Prayers of Sherkin,* 1991

Ireland, sir, for good or evil, is like no other place under Heaven, and no man can touch its sod or breathe its air without becoming better or worse.

— GEORGE BERNARD SHAW, *John Bull's Other Island,* 1904

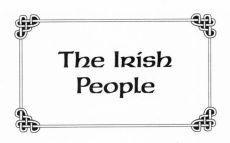

The Irish People

You are Irish you say lightly, and allocated to you are the tendencies to be wild, wanton, drunk, superstitious, unreliable, backward, toadying and prone to fits, whereas you know that in fact a whole entourage of ghosts resides in you, ghosts with whom the inner rapport is as frequent, as perplexing, as defiant as with any of the living.

—EDNA O'BRIEN, *Mother Ireland,* 1976

The great Gaels of Ireland
Are the men that God made mad,
For all their wars are merry,
And all their songs are sad.

—G. K. CHESTERTON, *The Ballad of the White Horse,* 1911

Irishness is not primarily a question of birth or blood or language; it is the condition of being involved in the Irish situation, and usually being mauled by it.

—Conor Cruise O'Brien, "Irishness,"
New Statesman, January 1959

The Irishman is one of the world's puzzles. People seem to be quite unable to agree as to who he is, or as to what constitutes his Irishness. Some people say that he is a Celt. Some say he is a Catholic. Some say he is a comic person. Some say he is a melancholy person. Others say he is both. According to some, he is of a gay, generous nature. According to others, he is a shrivelled piece of miserliness and superstition. . . . The truth is, there is a great deal of nonsense talked about the "real Irishman" and the "typical Irishman"—to mention two phrases common among thoughtless people. The "real Irishman" is neither essentially a Celt nor essentially a Catholic. He is merely a man who has had the good or bad fortune to be born in Ireland or of Irish parents, and who is interested in Ireland more than in any other country in the world.

—Robert Lynd, *Home Life in Ireland,* 1909

We are one of the great stocks of Europe. We are the people of Burke; we are the people of Grattan; we are the people of Swift, the people of Emmet, the people of Parnell. We have created the most of the modern literature of this country. We have created the best of its political intelligence.

—W. B. YEATS, debate on divorce in the Seanad Éireann (the upper house of the Republic of Ireland Parliament), June 11, 1925

The Irish say your trouble is their trouble and your joy their joy? I wish I could believe it; I'm troubled, I'm dissatisfied, I'm Irish.

—MARIANNE MOORE, *Spenser's Ireland,* 1941

When anyone asks me about the Irish character, I say look at the trees, maimed, stark and misshapen, but ferociously tenacious.

—EDNA O'BRIEN

There's no point in being Irish if you don't know the world is going to break your heart eventually.

—DANIEL PATRICK MOYNIHAN, upon hearing the news of John F. Kennedy's assassination.

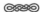

It's not that the Irish are cynical. It's simply that they have a wonderful lack of respect for everything and everybody.

—BRENDAN BEHAN

The Irish are a fair people;—they never speak well of one another.

—SAMUEL JOHNSON, *Life of Samuel Johnson* by Boswell, 1791

When the soul of a man is born in this country, there are nets flung at it to hold it back from flight. You talk to me of nationality, language, religion. I shall try to fly by those nets.

—JAMES JOYCE, *A Portrait of the Artist as a Young Man,* 1916

I showed my appreciation of my native land in the usual Irish way: by getting out of it as soon as I possibly could.

— GEORGE BERNARD SHAW

That's the Irish people all over—they treat a joke as a serious thing and a serious thing as a joke.

—SEAN O'CASEY, *The Shadow of a Gunman,* 1923

My one claim to originality among Irishmen is that I have never made a speech.

— GEORGE MOORE

I like to do all the talking myself. It saves time, and prevents arguments.

— OSCAR WILDE

The Irish People

We've never been cool, we're hot. Irish people are Italians who can't dress, Jamaicans who can't dance.

—BONO, February 2001

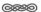

Other people have a nationality. The Irish and the Jews have a psychosis.

—BRENDAN BEHAN, *Richard's Cork Leg,* 1964

We are ashamed of everything that is real about us; ashamed of ourselves, of our relatives, of our incomes, of our accents, of our opinions, of our experience, just as we are ashamed of our naked skins.

—GEORGE BERNARD SHAW, *Man and Superman,* 1903

This is one race of people for whom psychoanalysis is of no use whatsoever.

—SIGMUND FREUD

The hospitality of an Irishman is not the running account
of posted and ledgered courtesies, as in other countries; it
springs, like all his qualities, his faults, his virtues, directly
from his heart.

—DANIEL O'CONNELL, speech against Marquess of Headfort,
July 1804

Old Days! The wild geese are flighting,
Head to the storm as they faced it before!
For where there are Irish there's loving and fighting,
And when we stop either, it's Ireland no more!

—RUDYARD KIPLING, *The Irish Guards,* 1918

We Irish are too poetical to be poets; we are a nation of
brilliant failures, but we are the greatest talkers since
the Greeks.

—OSCAR WILDE, remark to young W. B. Yeats in London,
quoted in *The Anglo-Irish* by Terence de Vere White, 1972

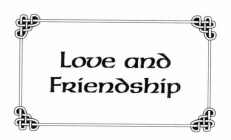

Love and Friendship

The story of a love is not important—what is important is that one is capable of love. It is perhaps the only glimpse we are permitted of eternity.

—HELEN HAYES

No, there's nothing half so sweet in life
As love's young dream.

—THOMAS MOORE, "Love's Young Dream"

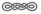

A pity beyond all telling,
Is hid in the heart of love:

—W. B. YEATS, "The Pity of Love," 1891

Cleopatra: All people are strangers and enemies to us except those we love.

— GEORGE BERNARD SHAW, *Caesar and Cleopatra,* 1899

It isn't human to love, you know. It's foolish, it's a folly, a divine folly. It's beyond all reason, all limits.

— SEAN O'FAOLAIN, "Lovers of the Lake," 1957

Love is a very strange idea. I never know what it is. When you were young it seemed to be all intensity and no opportunity. Later when you did have the opportunity the fire had gone out of it.

— BERNARD MACLAVERTY, *Cal,* 1983

To love oneself is the beginning of a lifelong romance.

— OSCAR WILDE, *An Ideal Husband,* 1895

Promiscuity is the death of love.

—EDNA O'BRIEN, radio interview with Michael Krasny,
October 16, 1995

⊙∞⊙

The fickleness of the women whom I love is only equaled by
the infernal constancy of the women who love me.

— GEORGE BERNARD SHAW, *The Philanderer,* 1893

⊙∞⊙

Sometimes I wonder if men and women really suit each other.
Perhaps they should live next door and just visit now and then.

—KATHERINE HEPBURN

⊙∞⊙

Keep love in your heart. A life without it is like a sunless
garden when the flowers are dead. The consciousness of
loving and being loved brings a warmth and richness to life
that nothing else can bring.

— OSCAR WILDE

The hours I spend with you I look upon as sort of a perfumed garden, a dim twilight, and a fountain singing to it . . . you and you alone make me feel that I am alive . . . Other men it is said have seen angels, but I have seen thee and thou art enough.

— GEORGE MOORE, letter to Lady Emerald Cunard,
quoted in *The Everything Wedding Vows Book*, edited by
Janet Anastasio and Michelle Bevilacqua, 2001

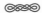

To be in love is to surpass oneself.

— OSCAR WILDE, *The Picture of Dorian Gray*, 1891

Yet each man kills the thing he loves,
By each let this be heard,
Some do it with a bitter look,
Some with a flattering word.
The coward does it with a kiss,
The brave man with a sword!

— OSCAR WILDE, *The Ballad of Reading Gaol*, 1898

Love is never defeated, and I could add, the history of Ireland proves it.

—POPE JOHN PAUL II, *speech to people of Galway, September 1979*

It is in the thirties that we want friends. In the forties we know they won't save us any more than love did.

—F. SCOTT FITZGERALD, "The Note-Books," *The Crack-Up,*
edited by Edmund Wilson, 1931

Anybody can sympathise with the sufferings of a friend, but it requires a very fine nature—it requires, in fact, the nature of a true individualist— to sympathise with a friend's success.

—OSCAR WILDE, "The Soul of Man Under Socialism,"
Fortnightly Review, February 1891

I'm sittin' on the stile, Mary,
Where we sat side by side.
I'm very lonely now, Mary,
For the poor make no new friends.

—LADY HELEN SELINA, Lady Dufferin, "Lament of the Irish Emigrant"

Forsake not a friend of many years for an acquaintance of a day.

—IRISH PROVERB

Oh, call it by some better name,
For Friendship sounds too cold,
While love is now a worldly flame,
Whose shrine must be of gold;
And Passion like, the sun at noon,
That burns o'er all he sees
Awhile as warm, will set as soon—
Then, call it none of these.
Imagine something purer far,
More free from stain of clay
Than Friendship, Love or Passion are,
Yet human still as they;
And if thy lip, for love like this
No mortal word can frame,
Go, ask of angels what it is,
And call it by that name.

—THOMAS MOORE

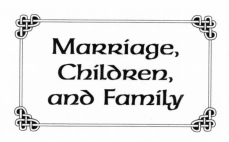

Marriage, Children, and Family

When two people are under the influence of the most violent, most insane, most delusive, and most transient of passions, they are required to swear that they will remain in that excited, abnormal, and exhausting condition continuously until death do them part.

— George Bernard Shaw, *Getting Married*, 1908

All that a husband or wife really wants is to be pitied a little, praised a little, appreciated a little.

— Oliver Goldsmith

A successful marriage requires falling in love many times, always with the same person.

— Mignon McLaughlin

I said, "Miss O'Connell" (she was also an O'Connell) "are you engaged?" She replied, "I am not!" I said, "Then will you engage yourself to me?" "I will," was her reply; and I said I would devote my life to make her happy. She deserved that I should. She gave me thirty-four years of the purest happiness that man ever enjoyed.

—DANIEL O'CONNELL, on the death of his wife, October 31, 1836

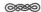

So they were married—to be the more together—
And found they were never again so much together
Divided by the morning tea,
By the evening paper,
By children and tradesmen's bills.

—LOUIS MACNEICE, *Plant and Phantom*, 1941

The marriage state, with and without the affection suitable to it, is the completest image of Heaven and Hell we are capable of receiving in this life.

—SIR RICHARD STEELE

Marriage is popular because it combines the maximum of temptation with the maximum of opportunity.

— GEORGE BERNARD SHAW, *Maxims for Revolutionists,* 1903

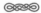

Matrimony is the only game of chance the clergy favor.

—EMILY FERGUSON MURPHY

Love—but not marriage. Marriage means a four-post bed and papa and mamma between eleven and twelve. Love is aspiration: transparencies, colour, light, a sense of the unreal. But a wife—you know all about her—who her father was, who her mother was, what she thinks of you and her opinion of the neighbours over the way. Where, then, is the dream?

— GEORGE MOORE, *Confessions of a Young Man,* 1886

Call me pathetic . . . but I'm being honest here. I want a bloke, a partner, a long-term commitment. I want the M word.

—MARIAN KEYES, *Late Opening at the Last Chance Saloon,* 2003

For an artist to marry his model is as fatal as for a gourmet to marry his cook: the one gets no sittings, and the other gets no dinners.

— OSCAR WILDE, "London Models,"
The English Illustrated Magazine, January 1889

Woman begins by resisting a man's advances and ends by blocking his retreat.

— OSCAR WILDE, *An Ideal Husband,* 1895

We do not squabble, fight or have rows. We collect grudges. We're in an arms race, storing up warheads for the domestic Armageddon.

—HUGH LEONARD, *Time Was,* 1980

There's nothing in the world like the devotion of a married woman. It's a thing no married man knows anything about.

— OSCAR WILDE, *Lady Windermere's Fan,* 1892

Forbearance towards errors and defects, and a just appreciation of good qualities, joined to mildness and good breeding, is what we would inculcate as the surest means of preserving domestic harmony, and of promoting domestic affection.

—MARGUERITE POWER, Countess of Blessington,
The Repealers, 1834

Another point of importance is their children not being burthensome. In all the enquiries I made into the state of the poor, I found their happiness and ease generally relative to the number of their children, and nothing considered as such a misfortune as having none.

—ARTHUR YOUNG, *A Tour in Ireland*, 1780

Parentage is a very important profession, but no test of fitness for it is ever imposed in the interest of the children.

—GEORGE BERNARD SHAW,
Everybody's Political What's What?, 1944

Don't set your wit against a child.

—JONATHAN SWIFT, adapted from *Polite Conversation*

Whenever I held my newborn baby in my arms, I used to think that what I said and did to him could have an influence not only on him but on all whom he met, not only for a day or a month or a year, but for all eternity—a very, very challenging and exciting thought for a mother.

—ROSE KENNEDY, quoted in *Rose: A Biography of Rose Fitzgerald Kennedy* by Gail Cameron, 1971

The real menace in dealing with a five-year-old is that in no time at all you begin to sound like a five-year-old.

—JEAN KERR, *Please Don't Eat the Daisies,* 1957

My mother took too much, a great deal too much, care of me; she over-educated, over-instructed, over-dosed me with premature lessons of prudence: she was so afraid that I should ever do a foolish thing, or not say a wise one, that she prompted my every word, and guided my eyes, hearing with her ears, and judging with her understanding, till, at length, it was found out that I had no eyes, or understanding of my own.

—MARIA EDGEWORTH, *Vivian,* 1812

I am what her savage loving has made me.

—SAMUEL BECKETT, about his mother,
quoted in *Damned to Fame* by James Knowlson, 1996

Children begin by loving their parents; as they grow older
they judge them; sometimes they forgive them.

—OSCAR WILDE, *The Picture of Dorian Gray*, 1891

The best brought-up children are those who have seen their
parents as they are; hypocrisy is not the parent's first duty.

—GEORGE BERNARD SHAW, "The Revolutionist's Handbook," 1903

If you don't want your children to hear what you're saying,
pretend you're talking to them.

—E. C. MCKENZIE

The midwife said that the agony of having a child could last a long time. I didn't realize she meant eighteen years.

—SINEAD MURPHY

꧁꧂

Family love is messy, clinging, and of an annoying and repetitive pattern, like bad wallpaper.

—P. J. O'ROURKE, *Modern Manners*, 1994

꧁꧂

The worse misfortune that can happen to an ordinary man is to have an extraordinary father.

—AUSTIN O'MALLEY

꧁꧂

I do not think of you lying in the wet clay
of a Monaghan graveyard; I see
You walking down a lane among the poplars
On your way to the station, or happily
Going to a second Mass on a summer Sunday—

—PATRICK KAVANAGH, "In Memory of My Mother"

I am their wall against all danger,
Their door against the wind and snow,
Thou Whom a woman laid in manger
Take me not till the children grow!

—KATHARINE TYNAN, "Any Woman"

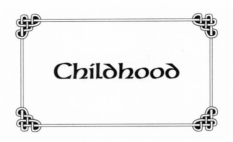

Childhood

Like all children, I led a double life. There was the ordinariness of dressing in the morning, putting on shoes and combing hair, stirring a spoon through porridge I didn't want, and going at ten to nine to the nuns' elementary school. And there was a world in which only the events I wished for happened, where boredom was not permitted and of which I was both God and King.

—WILLIAM TREVOR, "The Death of Peggy Meehan," *Great Irish Stories of Childhood* edited by Peter Haining, 1997

When I look back on my childhood I wonder how I managed to survive it at all. It was, of course, a miserable childhood: the happy childhood is hardly worth your while. Worse than the ordinary miserable childhood is the miserable Irish childhood, and worse yet is the miserable Irish Catholic childhood.

—FRANK MCCOURT, *Angela's Ashes,* 1996

Childhood

Violence alone enlivened my girlhood, for I was allowed out only to go to school and mass.

—MARY COSTELLO, *Titanic Town*, 2000

One master will hit you if you don't know that Eamon de Valera is the greatest man that ever lived. Another master will hit you if you don't know that Michael Collins was the greatest man that ever lived . . . If you ever say anything good about Oliver Cromwell they'll all hit you.

—FRANK MCCOURT, *Angela's Ashes*, 1996

I remember coming out of St. Patrick's, Sunday after Sunday, strained almost to torture by the music, and walking out through the slums of Harold's Cross as the lamps were being lit. Hordes of wild children used to play round the cathedral of St. Patrick and I remember there was something appalling— a proximity of emotions as conflicting as the perversions of the Black Mass—in coming out suddenly from the white harmonies of the Passion according to St. Matthew among this blasphemy of childhood.

—JOHN MILLINGTON SYNGE, *Autobiography*, 1966

Well, before we'd go to school, we'd have a lot of work to
be done. We'd have to go to the well for drinking water. . . .
And there was turnips and mangels to be put through the
grinder—that also had to be turned by hand. So each one of us
got jobs to do. Another one might be feeding the calves before
breakfast, which would consist of porridge, or stirabout as we
called it, soda bread and homemade butter. Then for school,
we'd take some cuts of bread and butter and maybe a cut of
sweet cake as well. All wrapped up with a bottle of milk. We
had to be at school for half nine, so it would take us, oh, an
hour at least to cover that distance—six or seven miles.

—JIM HICKEY, *Irish Days: Oral Histories of the Twentieth Century*
edited by Margaret Hickey, 2001

In those days, and it was only in the 1950s, when children
were fifteen years old, the law allowed them to leave school
if they wanted to, and get a job. I recall being dismayed,
having suggested the idea to my parents, at their horror. They
instructed me to forget such ridiculous notions, for I would
stay on at school and, hopefully, go on to higher education.

—PETER TREMAYNE, "The Way of the White Cow," in *Great Irish
Stories of Childhood* edited by Peter Haining, 1997

Childhood

Children were toughened early, sent out into the world with their cardboard suitcases—one minute warm in the tribe, the next minute walking down the steps of some distant railway station into a world they must handle on their own.

—NUALA O'FAOLAIN, *Are You Somebody?*, 1996

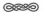

I was fourteen, and abruptly at the end of the holidays some soft, almost physical appendage of childhood seemed to have fallen away, like the tail of a tadpole, and I would never be quite the same again.

—VAL MULKERNS, "Home for Christmas"

We hear a great deal of lamentation these days about writers having all taken themselves to the colleges and universities where they live decorously instead of going out and getting firsthand information about life. The fact is that anybody who has survived his childhood has enough information about life to last him the rest of his days.

—FLANNERY O'CONNOR, *Mystery and Manners*, 1969

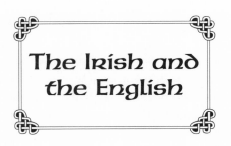

The Irish and
the English

England and Ireland may flourish together. The world is large enough for us both. Let it be our care not to make ourselves too little for it.

—EDMUND BURKE, letter to Samuel Span

I defy anyone to study Irish history without getting a dislike and distrust of England.

—LADY ISABELLA AUGUSTA GREGORY

The moment the very name of Ireland is mentioned, the English seem to bid adieu to common feeling, common prudence, and common sense, and to act with the barbarity of tyrants, and the fatuity of idiots.

—SYDNEY SMITH, *Letters of Peter Plymley*, 1808

The Irish and the English

When the historian of this troubled reign turns to Ireland, his task becomes peculiarly difficult and delicate. His steps—to borrow the fine image used on a similar occasion by a Roman poet—are on the thin crust of ashes, beneath which the lava is still glowing.

—THOMAS BABINGTON MACAULAY,
History of England from the Accession of James II, 1849

A rich land and a poor people. I ask you a question. Why is this?

—HUMPHREY O'SULLIVAN,
The Diary of an Irish Countryman, 1827–1835

Thus you have a starving population, an absentee aristocracy, and an alien Church, and in addition the weakest executive in the world. That is the Irish Question.

—BENJAMIN DISRAELI, speech in the House of Commons,
February 16, 1844

Because a man is born in a stable, that does not make him a horse.

—DUKE OF WELLINGTON, rejecting his Irish roots

Why should Ireland be treated as a geographical fragment
of England...? Ireland is not a geographical fragment. She is
a nation.

— CHARLES STEWART PARNELL

The English always have their wars in someone else's country.

—BRENDAN BEHAN, *The Wit of Brendan Behan,*
compiled by Sean McCann, 1968

We have always found the Irish a bit odd. They refuse to
be English.

—WINSTON CHURCHILL

> Don't be surprised
> If I demur, for, be advised
> My passport's green.
> No glass of ours was ever raised
> To toast the Queen.

—SEAMUS HEANY, responding in an open letter to the editors of
Penguin Book of Contemporary British Poetry
for including him as a contributor, 1982

Could he not find in his heart the generosity to acknowledge that there is a small nation that stood alone not for one year or two, but for several hundred years against aggression; that endured spoliations, famines, massacres in endless succession; that was clubbed many times into insensibility, but that each time on returning [to] consciousness took up the fight anew; a small nation that could never be got to accept defeat and has never surrendered her soul?

—EAMON DE VALERA, radio broadcast, in response to criticism by Winston Churchill of Ireland's neutrality in World War II, May 8, 1945

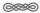

We've been waiting seven hundred years, you can have the seven minutes.

—MICHAEL COLLINS, after being told he was seven minutes late to arrive at Dublin Castle for the handover by British forces on January 16, 1922, quoted in *Michael Collins* by Tim Pat Coogan, 1990

It is a curious contradiction, not very often remembered in England, that for many generations the private soldiers of the British Army were largely Irish.

— CECIL WOODHAM-SMITH, *The Great Hunger: Ireland, 1845–1849*

I prefer to live in Ireland, but I've a great admiration for the British people. No one else could have used Churchill so well during the war and then thrown him out at the right time afterwards.

—BRENDAN BEHAN, *The Wit of Brendan Behan*
compiled by Sean McCann, 1968

❦

It seems that the historic inability in Britain to comprehend Irish feelings and sensitivities still remains.

— CHARLES HAUGHEY, quoted in *The Observer,* February 1988

❦

The Irish are still the people the English understand least. And we're just not sure ... if they will ever really forgive us for the unspeakable sin of not wanting to be like them.

—JOSEPH O'CONNOR, *The Secret World of the Irish Male,* 1994

Madam President, speaking here in Dublin Castle it is impossible to ignore the weight of history. . . . Indeed, so much of this visit reminds us of the complexity of our history, its many layers and traditions, but also the importance of forbearance and conciliation. Of being able to bow to the past, but not be bound by it. Of course, the relationship has not always been straightforward; nor has the record over the centuries been entirely benign. It is a sad and regrettable reality that through our history our islands have experienced more than their fair share of heartache, turbulence, and loss. . . . But it is also true that no one who looked to the future over the past centuries could have imagined the strength of the bonds that are now in place between the governments and the people of our two nations, the spirit of partnership that we now enjoy, and the lasting rapport between us. No one here this evening could doubt that heartfelt desire of our two nations. . . . What were once only hopes for the future have now come to pass; it is almost exactly 13 years since the overwhelming majority of people in Ireland and Northern Ireland voted in favour of the agreement signed on Good Friday 1998, paving the way for Northern Ireland to become the exciting and inspirational place that it is today.

— QUEEN ELIZABETH II's speech at Dublin Castle State Dinner, May 18, 2011

It is only right that on this historic visit we should reflect on the difficult centuries which have brought us to this point. Inevitably where there are the colonisers and the colonised, the past is a repository of sources of bitter division. The harsh facts cannot be altered nor loss nor grief erased, but with time and generosity, interpretations and perspectives can soften and open up space for new accommodations.

—MARY MCALEESE, speech at Dublin Castle State Dinner in honor of Queen Elizabeth II, May 18, 2011

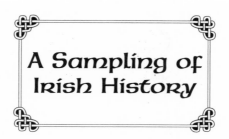

A Sampling of Irish History

The actual course of Irish history from the late sixteenth century to the end of the eighteenth, provides abundant material for history lessons.... All you have to do is leave out the atrocities committed by your own side, and provide copious details of those committed by the enemy. Thus Protestant historians exaggerated the atrocities committed by Catholics against Protestants in the rebellion of 1641, and minimised or justified the massacres of Catholics by Cromwell's forces eight years later. Catholic historians pounced on the Protestant exaggerations of 1641, and ignored, or played down the Catholic atrocities which had actually occurred. Cromwell's atrocities, on the other hand, got from Catholics the kind of attention Protestants devoted to 1641. All political and religious zealots everywhere do this kind of thing instinctively.

— CONOR CRUISE O'BRIEN, *Ancestral Voices*, 1994

To unite the whole people of Ireland, to abolish the memory
of all past dissension and to substitute the common name
of Irishman in place of the denominations of Protestant,
Catholic, and Dissenter—these were my means.

—THEOBALD WOLFE TONE, in August 1796

Poor Croppies, ye know your sentence has come,
When you heard the dread sound of the Protestant drum.
In memory of William we hoisted the flag
And soon the bright Orange put down the Green rag.

—Anonymous Protestant loyalist folk-song
dating from 1798 rebellion

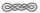

Until, on Vinegar Hill, the final conclave.
Terraced thousands died, shaking scythes at cannon.

—SEAMUS HEANEY, "Requiem for the Croppies," 1969

The one great principle of any settlement of the Irish question
must be the recognition of the divine right of Irish men, and
Irish men alone, to rule Ireland.

—JOHN REDMOND, speech, Chicago, August 1886

I have but a few more words to say . . . I am going to my cold and silent grave—my lamp of life is nearly extinguished, my race is run—the grave opens to receive me, and I sink into its bosom. I have but one request to make at my departure from this world; it is the charity of its silence. Let no man write my epitaph; for as no man who knows my motives dare now vindicate them, let not prejudice or ignorance asperse them. Let them rest in obscurity and peace! Let my memory be left in oblivion, my tomb remain uninscribed, until other times and other men can do justice to my character. When my country takes her place among the nations of the earth, *then*, and *not till then*, let my epitaph be written.

—ROBERT EMMET, speech after hearing he'd been sentenced to death for treason, 1803

Oh, Ireland! thou emerald of the ocean, whose sons are generous and brave, whose daughters are honourable and frank and fair, thou art the isle on whose green shores I have desired to see the standard of liberty erected—a flag of fire— a beacon at which the world shall light the torch of Freedom!

—PERCY BYSSHE SHELLEY, "An Address to the Irish People," 1812

Apostles of Freedom are ever idolised when dead, but crucified when alive.

—JAMES CONNOLLY, *Workers Republic,* August 1898

∞∞∞

Ireland unfree shall never be at peace.

—PATRICK PEARSE, August 1915

∞∞∞

People say: "Of course, they will be beaten." The statement is almost a query, and they continue, "but they are putting up a decent fight." For being beaten does not matter greatly in Ireland, but not fighting does matter.

—JAMES STEPHENS, *The Insurrection in Dublin,* 1916

∞∞∞

Be green upon their graves. O happy Spring!
For they were young and eager who are dead!
Of all things that are young, and quivering
With eager life, be they rememberéd!

—JAMES STEPHENS, "Spring—1916"

You must not grieve for all this. We have preserved Ireland's honour and our own. Our deeds of last week are the most splendid in Ireland's history. People will say hard things of us now, but we shall be remembered by posterity and blessed by unborn generations. You too will be blessed because you were my mother.

—PATRICK PEARSE, letter to his mother from prison following the Easter Rising, May 1916

I write it out in a verse—
MacDonagh and MacBride
And Connolly and Pearse
Now and in time be,
Wherever green is worn,
Are changed, changed utterly:
A terrible beauty is born.

—W. B. YEATS, "Easter, 1916," 1921

An Irishman resorting to arms to achieve the independence of his country is only doing what Englishmen would do if it were their misfortune to be invaded and conquered by the Germans in the course of the war.

— GEORGE BERNARD SHAW, letter, April 1916

It is absolutely impossible to slaughter a man in this position without making him a martyr and a hero, even though the day before the rising he may have been only a minor poet.

— GEORGE BERNARD SHAW, letter to *The Daily News*,
London, May 10, 1916

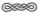

Where all your rights become only an accumulated wrong; where men must beg with bated breath for leave to subsist in their own land, to think their own thoughts, to sing their own songs, to garner the fruits of their own labours ... then surely it is a braver, a saner and truer thing, to be a rebel in act and deed against such circumstances as these than tamely to accept it as the natural lot of men.

—ROGER CASEMENT, statement at the end of his trial,
the Old Bailey, London, June 29, 1916

The contest on our side is not one of rivalry or vengeance, but of endurance. It is not those who can inflict the most, but those who can suffer the most who will conquer.

—TERENCE MACSWINEY, inaugural speech after being
elected Mayor of Cork in March 1920
(MacSwiney died on hunger strike on October 25, 1920.)

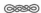

The years from 1918 to 1923 were to be dramatic ones throughout Ireland. They were to see the ousting of the old Home Rule Party (UIL) by Sinn Fein, the establishment of an illegal Irish parliament in Dublin in defiance of Westminster, and the outbreak of a War of Independence against British rule in Ireland. In the North the violent confrontation between Unionist and Nationalist which had been looming for so long was finally to erupt. The outcome would be partial independence for the bulk of the country in the new Irish Free State, and partition leaving the six north-eastern counties under the British rule in the United Kingdom—but with local self-government.

—MICHAEL FARRELL, *Northern Ireland: The Orange State*, 1976

There is no crime in detecting and destroying in war-time, the spy and the informer. They have destroyed without trial. I have paid them back in their own coin.

—MICHAEL COLLINS, private document on Bloody Sunday,
quoted in *Michael Collins* by Rex Taylor, 1958

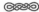

Think—what I have got for Ireland? Something which she has wanted these past seven hundred years. Will anyone be satisfied with the bargain? Will anyone? I tell you this—early this morning I signed my death warrant. I thought at the time how odd, how ridiculous—a bullet may just as well have done the job five years ago.

—MICHAEL COLLINS, from a December 6, 1921, letter to John O'Kane
on signing the treaty with Great Britain establishing the Irish Free
State, quoted in *Michael Collins and the Treaty* by T. R. Dwyer, 1981

So tear up your mourning and hang up your brightest colours in his honour; and let us all praise God that he had not to die in a snuffy bed of a trumpery cough, weakened by age, and saddened by the disappointments that would have attended his work had he lived.

—GEORGE BERNARD SHAW, letter to Michael Collins's sister, Johanna,
August 24, 1922

There are in every generation those who shrink from the ultimate sacrifice, but there are in every generation those who make it with joy and laughter and these are the salt of the generations.

—PATRICK PEARSE, Robert Emmet Commemoration Address, Brooklyn, NY, March 2, 1914

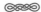

Whenever I wanted to know what the Irish people wanted, I had only to examine my own heart and it told me straight off what the Irish people wanted.

—EAMON DE VALERA, address to the Dáil Éireann (the lower house of the Irish Parliament), January 6, 1922

[Our prejudices are] so deeply rooted that we never think of them as prejudices but call them common sense.

— GEORGE BERNARD SHAW, *The Intelligent Woman's Guide to Socialism, Capitalism, Sovietism and Fascism,* 1928

You cannot talk peace until the enemy surrenders, and the enemy is the Roman Catholic Church.

—IAN PAISLEY, quoted in *The Irish Times,* August 23, 1969

In my experience, people of Planter stock often suffer from some crisis of identity, of not knowing where they belong. Among us you will find some who call themselves British, some Irish, some Ulstermen, usually with a degree of hesitation or mental fumbling.

—JOHN HEWITT, "No Rootless Colonist," 1972

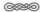

Belfast . . . seemed to have gone berserk. On the news we heard that there were gunfights raging in the Falls, the Markets, Ardoyne, Andersonstown and New Lodge Road. There were many dead. Protestant crowds had joined in the fighting, backing the army up. Whole streets were burning and thousands of refugees began to flee to the South. The twenty-four hours after internment were the bloodiest Northern Ireland had known for decades.

—EAMONN MCCANN, *War and an Irish Town*, 1973

It was a typical "Ulster" conversation, with gaps and deliberate omissions reaching right back to the Boyne and the Penal Laws. Better keep your mouth shut and no harm done.

—DENIS IRELAND, *From the Jungle of Belfast*, 1973

I have never and never will accept the right of a minority who happen to be a majority in a small part of the country to opt out of a nation.

—JACK LYNCH, quoted in the *Irish Times,* November 14, 1970

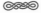

My heart besieged by anger, my mind a gap of danger,
I walked among their old haunts, the home ground where
    they bled;
And in the dirt lay justice like an acorn in the winter
Till its oak would sprout in Derry where the thirteen men
    lay dead.

—SEAMUS HEANEY, "The Road to Derry," about the Bloody Sunday
massacre in Londonderry, January 30, 1972

The three components of Unionism are British heritage, Protestantism and supremacy. British heritage and Protestantism they should have, a man is entitled to his heritage, but supremacy they cannot have, any more than the Boer can in South Africa.

—TIM PAT COOGAN, interview in the
Irish-Australian Newspaper, 1996

I feel like an exile at heart—the call of the North is always there.

—MARY MCALEESE, *Irish Times,* September 2, 1997

⊚⟨⟨⟨⟩⟩⟩⊚

From the depths of my heart I believe Northern Ireland has come to a time of peace, a time when hate will no longer rule.

—IAN PAISELY, following his historic swearing-in as First Minister of the power-sharing government of Northern Ireland, May 2007

⊚⟨⟨⟨⟩⟩⟩⊚

Peace cannot be built on exclusion. That has been the price of the past 30 years.

—GERRY ADAMS, *Daily Telegraph,* April 11, 1998

⊚⟨⟨⟨⟩⟩⟩⊚

It is a day we should treasure. Today is about the promise of a bright future, a day when we hope a line will be drawn under the bloody past.

—BERTIE AHERN, *The Guardian,* April 11, 1998

I am pleased to announce that the two governments and the political parties in Northern Ireland have reached agreement.

— GEORGE MITCHELL, *The Times*, April 11, 1998

The settlement shows that the will of the people for peace and co-operation is stronger than the divide.

—JACQUES SANTER, *The Times*, April 11, 1998

The people have spoken and the politicians have had to listen.

— GERRY FITT, on the result of the referendum on the Good Friday agreement, *Sunday Telegraph*, May 24, 1998

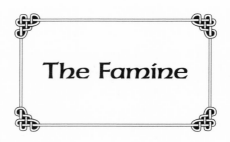

The Famine

From 1782 on, and especially during the Napoleonic wars, when Ireland had become the granary of England, the country had passed through a period of great prosperity. Taking advantage of this, the landlords had multiplied the number of small holdings on their estates, as by this subdivision they increased the number of their voters and raised the total of their rents. As a result, the population increased rapidly, and continued to increase notwithstanding a gradual change in economic conditions. On the conclusion of the war the rise in prices was succeeded by a fall. Tillage ceased to pay, and the landlords were naturally tempted to turn the agricultural lands into pasture. A campaign of "Clearances" was inaugurated and continued without intermission. It became especially vigorous when by the Act of 1829 the smaller peasants were deprived of the right of voting. The tenantry were driven out, and their houses razed to the ground. Holdings were "consolidated." Parliament looked on complacently, and passed laws to make ejectment an inexpensive process. As there were no industries to relieve the pressure, the people crowded in upon such remnants of the soil as were left to them. They were compelled to pay famine rents, which, as John Stuart Mill put it, scarcely left them enough to stave off death from starvation. They lived on potatoes as the Chinese lived on rice. Were a bad harvest to come a catastrophe must inevitably ensue.

There came not one bad harvest, but three in succession. In the autumn of 1845 three-quarters of the potato crop was destroyed in a few days by a form of blight hitherto unknown. In 1846 and 1847 the whole potato crop perished. From 1846 to 1849 famine reigned throughout the land. No sooner did the plague touch them than the people seemed plunged in a sort of stupor.

It was no uncommon sight to see the cottier and his little family seated on the garden fence gazing all day long in moody silence at the blighted plot that had been their last hope. Nothing would rouse them. You spoke: they answered not; you tried to cheer them: they shook their heads.

—L. PAUL-DUBOIS, *Contemporary Ireland,* 1908

Families, when all was eaten and no hope left, took their last look at the sun, built up their cottage doors, that none might see them die nor hear their groans, and were found weeks afterwards, skeletons on their own hearth.

—JOHN MITCHEL, *Jail Journal,* 1914

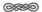

Take it from us, every grain,
We were made for your to drain;
Black starvation let us feel,
England must not want a meal!
When our rotting roots shall fail,
When the hunger pangs assail,
Ye'll have of Irish corn your fill—
We'll have grass and nettles still!

—JOHN O'HAGAN, "Famine and Exportation"

A plague-wind blew across the land,
Fever was in the air,
Fields were black that once were green
And death was everywhere.

—M. J. MACMANUS, "1849"

The Famine

There's famine in the land, its grip is tightening still!
There's trouble, black and bitter, on every side I glance,
There are dead upon the roadside, and dead upon the hill,
But my Jamie's safe and well away in France.

—EMILY LAWLESS, "An Exile's Mother"

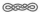

This girl was poor; she hadn't a home
Or a single thing she could call her own,
Drifting about in the saddest of lives
Doing odd jobs for other men's wives,
As if for drudgery created,
Begging a crust from a woman she hated.

—NINETEENTH-CENTURY IRISH SONG, quoted in *Remembering Ahanagran: A History of Stories* by Richard White, 1998

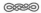

The Famine left hatred behind. Between Ireland and England the memory of what was done and endured has lain like a sword. Other famines followed, as other famines had gone before, but it is the terrible years of the Great Hunger which are remembered, and only just beginning to be forgiven.

—CECIL WOODHAM-SMITH, *The Great Hunger,* 1962

And they did perish; perished by hundreds, by thousands, by tens of thousands, by hundreds of thousands; perished in the houses, in the fields, by the roadside, in the ditches; perished from hunger, from cold, but most of all from famine-fever. It is an appalling picture, that which springs up to memory. Gaunt spectres move here and there, looking at one another out of hollow eyes of despair and gloom. Ghosts walk the land. Great giant figures, reduced to skeletons by hunger, shake in their clothes, which hang loose around their attenuated frames. Mothers try to still their children's cries of hunger by bringing their cold, blue lips to milkless breasts. Here and there by the wayside a corpse stares at the passers-by, as it lies against the hedge where it sought shelter.

—PATRICK AUGUSTINE SHEEHAN, *Glenanaar*, 1905

Let us not dare to forget the terrible death and suffering that occurred between 1845 and 1850. In fact we should indelibly fix it in our personal and collective memory, for we are our ancestors.

—JANE WILDE, Irish poet and mother of Oscar Wilde

Those who governed in London at the time failed their people through standing by while a crop failure turned into a massive human tragedy. We must not forget such a dreadful event. It is also right that we should pay tribute to the ways in which the Irish people have triumphed in the face of this catastrophe.

—TONY BLAIR, official statement read at the Famine commemoration at Millstreet, County Cork, June 1, 1997

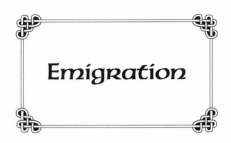

Emigration

It used to seem to me a very sad thing to see all the people going to America; the poor Celt disappearing in America, leaving his own country, leaving his language, and very often his religion.

— GEORGE MOORE, "A Play-House in the Waste," 1903

A man travels the world over in search of what he needs and returns home to find it.

— GEORGE MOORE, *The Brook Kerith,* 1916

No longer shall our children, like our cattle, be brought up for export.

— EAMON DE VALERA, address to the Dáil Éireann,
December 19, 1934

I was born here. My children were born here. What the hell do I have to do to be called an American?

—JOSEPH P. KENNEDY

⚬⚭⚭⚬

It took 115 years and 6,000 miles and three generations to make this trip, but I'm proud to be here.

—JOHN F. KENNEDY, speech at New Ross, Wexford, while visiting Ireland, 1963

⚬⚭⚭⚬

There must be something secretly catastrophic about a country from which so many people go, escape, and that something alongside the economic exigencies that sent over a million people in coffin ships when a blight hit the potato crops in 1847 and has been sending them in considerable numbers ever since.

—EDNA O'BRIEN, *Mother Ireland*, 1976

I remember still with emotion the emigration of the young
people of the neighbourhood to America.... The night before
their departure there would be a farewell gathering called an
American wake in one of the houses of the emigrating boys
or girls. There would be singing and dancing interlarded with
tears and lamentations until the early hours of the morning,
when, without sleep, the young people started for the train,
the mothers sometimes keening as at a funeral or a wake for
the dead, for the parting would often be forever and the
parents might never again see the boy or girl who was
crossing the ocean.

—MARY COLUM, *Life and the Dream,* 1947

I want to go to the Leinster hills,
To the Dublin hills by the rocky shore.
I want to climb to Ben-Edar's heights—
I want to be home once more.

—DORA SIGERSON SHORTER, *The Sad Years,* 1918

Emigration

An Irish boy was leaving
Leaving his native home
Crossing the broad Atlantic
Once more he wished to roam
And as he was leaving his mother
Who was standing on the quay
She threw her arms around his waist
And this to him did say

A mother's love's a blessing
No matter where you roam
Keep her while she's living
You'll miss her when she's gone
Love her as in childhood
Though feeble, old and grey
For you'll never miss a mother's love
Till she's buried beneath the clay.

—THOMAS P. KEENAN, "A Mother's Love Is a Blessing"

My feet are here on Broadway this blessed harvest morn,
But Oh the ache that's in them for the spot where I was born.

My weary hands are blistered from work in cold and heat,
And Oh to swing a scythe to-day, thro' fields of Irish wheat.

Had I the chance to wander back, or own a king's abode,
'Tis soon I'd see the hawthorn tree by the Old Bog Road.

—TERESA BRAYTON, "The Old Bog Road"

Eternal is the fact that the human creature born in Ireland and
brought up in its air is Irish. I have lived for twenty years in
Ireland and for seventy-two in England; but the twenty came
first, and in Britain I am still a foreigner and shall die one.

— GEORGE BERNARD SHAW, quoted in *Ireland in Mind*
edited by Alice Leccese Powers, 2000

Until recently, Irish-Americans, if they made money,
disappeared into wasp-dom in Connecticut.

—KEVIN WHELAN, *Irish Times,* June 1998

I was raised in an Irish-American home in Detroit where assimilation was the uppermost priority. The price of assimilation and respectability was amnesia. Although my great-grandparents were victims of the Great Hunger of the 1840s, even though I was named Thomas Emmet Hayden IV after the radical Irish exile Thomas Emmet, my inheritance was to be disinherited. My parents knew nothing of this past, or nothing worth passing on.

—TOM HAYDEN, *Irish on the Inside: In Search of the Soul of Irish America,* Tom Hayden, 2001

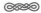

Being born Irish in America has become a privilege most of us take for granted. The days when "No Irish Need Apply" signs hung from every other job front are so distant that they shock our sun-protection-factor-55 ears upon retelling. We grew up in the shadow of Jack Kennedy and the Duke, drinking Guinness out of gas-powered cans while watching U2 perform live at Giants Stadium. We're cops, firemen, athletes, doctors, lawyers, bagmen, senators, presidents, and heads of state. Okay, so we still haven't had our own pope. But look on the bright side: neither have the French.

—DENIS LEARY, quoted in *Through Irish Eyes,* edited by Tracy Quinn, 1999

The country wears their going like a scar,
Today their relatives save to support and
Send others in planes for the new diaspora.

—SEAN DUNNE, "Letter from Ireland," 1991

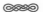

The immigrant's heart marches to the beat of two quite different drums, one from the old homeland and the other from the new. The immigrant has to bridge these two worlds, living comfortably in the new and bringing the best of his or her ancient identity and heritage to bear on life in an adopted homeland.

—MARY MCALEESE

I returned to Ireland. Ireland green and chaste and foolish. And when I wandered over my own hills and talked again to my own people I looked into the heart of this life and saw that it was good.

—PATRICK KAVANAGH, *The Green Fool,* 1938

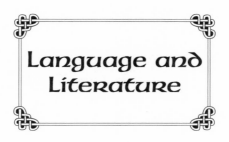

Language and Literature

A people without a language of its own is only half a nation. A nation should guard its language—'tis a surer barrier, and more important frontier, than fortress or river.

—THOMAS DAVIS, "The National Language," April 1843

To part with it would be to abandon a great part of ourselves, to lose the key of our past, to cut away the roots from the tree. With the language gone we could never aspire again to being more than half a nation.

—EAMON DE VALERA, radio broadcast on St. Patrick's Day, 1943

Everywhere in Irish prose there twinkles and peers the merry eye and laugh of a people who had little to laugh about in real life.

—DIARMUID RUSSELL, introduction to
The Portable Irish Reader, 1946

There is no language like the Irish for soothing and quieting.

—JOHN MILLINGTON SYNGE, *The Aran Islands*, 1907

I hear men and women of Connemara singing in the fields. Sounds go a long way in this still country. I hear the click of spade against stones and a voice lifted in some old Gaelic song. I would give anything to understand it. I have never wished to understand a foreign tongue so much.

—H. V. MORTON, *In Search of Ireland*, 1930

The English language brings out the best in the Irish. They court it like a beautiful woman. They make it bray with donkey laughter. They hurl it at the sky like a paint pot full of rainbows, and then make it chant a dirge for a man's fate and man's follies that is as mournful as misty spring rain crying over the fallow earth.

—T. E. KALEM, on Brendan Behan's 1958 play *Borstal Boy*, quoted in the *New York Times*, March 17, 1979

Although the Irish language is connected with many recollections which twine round the hearts of Irishmen, yet the superior utility of the English tongue as a medium of all modern communication is so great that I can witness without a sigh the gradual disuse of Irish.

—DANIEL O'CONNELL, *The Great Dan*
by Charles Chevenix Trench, 1984

If they really want to revive the Irish language, all they have to do is ban it.

—ANONYMOUS, quoted in *St. Patrick's People*
edited by Tony Gray, 1996

I am very sorry, but I cannot learn languages. I have tried hard, only to find that men of ordinary capacity can learn Sanskrit in less time than it takes me to buy a German dictionary.

— GEORGE BERNARD SHAW

We have really everything in common with America nowadays, except, of course, language.

— OSCAR WILDE, *The Canterville Ghost*, 1887

We make out of the quarrel with others, rhetoric, but of the quarrel with ourselves, poetry.

—W. B. YEATS, *Per Amica Silentia Lunae,* 1918

Poetry, even when apparently most fantastic, is always a revolt against artifice, a revolt, in a sense, against actuality.

—JAMES JOYCE, "James Clarence Mangan," 1902

Every good poem, in fact, is a bridge built from the known, familiar side of life over into the unknown. Science too, is always making expeditions into the unknown. But this does not mean that science can supersede poetry. For poetry enlightens us in a different way from science; it speaks directly to our feelings or imagination. The findings of poetry are no more and no less true than science.

—CECIL DAY-LEWIS, *Poetry for You,* 1944

That is what all poets do: they talk to themselves out loud; and the world overhears them. But it's horribly lonely not to hear someone else talk sometimes.

— GEORGE BERNARD SHAW, *Candida,* 1894

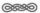

The point of poetry is to be acutely discomforting, to prod and provoke, to poke us in the eye, to punch us in the nose, to knock us off our feet, to take our breath away.

—PAUL MULDOON

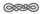

I can't think of a case where poems changed the world, but what they do is they change people's understanding of what's going on in the world.

— SEAMUS HEANEY

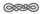

Literature always anticipates life. It does not copy it, but molds it to its purpose.

— OSCAR WILDE, "Sebastian Melmoth," *The Works of Oscar Wilde: Epigrams, Phrases and Philosophies for the Use of the Young,* 1909

I hate vulgar realism in literature. The man who could call a
spade a spade should be compelled to use one. It is the only
thing he is fit for.

> —OSCAR WILDE, *The Picture of Dorian Gray*, 1891

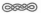

I haven't really written my plays and books—I've heard them.
The stories are there already, singing in your genes and in
your blood.

> —SEBASTIAN BARRY, *Irish Times*, February 19, 1998

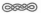

My real motive is to describe how my brain-damaged life is
as normal for me as my friends' able-bodied life is to them.
My mind is just like a spin-dryer at full speed; my thoughts
fly around my skull while millions of beautiful words cascade
down into my lap. Images gunfire across my consciousness and
while trying to discipline them I jump in awe at the soulfilled
bounty of my mind's expanse. Try then to imagine how
frustrating it is to give expression to that avalanche in efforts
of one great nod after the other.

> —CHRISTOPHER NOLAN, citing his reasons for writing
> *The Eye of the Clock*, quoted in *Observer*, November 8, 1987

Will you for Chrissake stop asking fellas if they read James Joyce's *Dubliners*. They're not interested. They're out for the night. Eat and drink all you can and leave James Joyce to blow his own trumpet.

—EDNA O'BRIEN, *The Lonely Girls,* 1962

❦

The difference between reality and fiction? Fiction has to make sense.

—TOM CLANCY, *SSN,* 2000

❦

The creations of a great writer are little more than the moods and passions of his own heart, given surnames and Christian names, and sent to walk the earth.

—W. B. YEATS

❦

The stories we tell determine the kind of history we make and remake.

—MARY ROBINSON, inaugural address, 1990

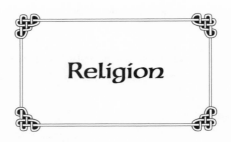

Religion

The time has long since gone when Irishmen and Irish women could be kept from thinking, by hurling priestly thunder at their heads.

—JAMES CONNOLLY, *Labour, Nationality, and Religion,* c. 1910

Man is by his constitution a religious animal; atheism is against not only our reason, but our instincts.

—EDMUND BURKE, *Reflections on the Revolution in France,* 1790

We have just enough religion to make us hate, but not enough to make us love one another.

—JONATHAN SWIFT, *Thoughts on Various Subjects,* 1711

Religion

I can't talk religion to a man with bodily hunger in his eyes.

— GEORGE BERNARD SHAW, *Major Barbara,* 1907

The Churches must learn humility as well as teach it.

— GEORGE BERNARD SHAW, Preface to *St. Joan,* 1923

Christianity might be a good thing if anyone ever tried it.

— GEORGE BERNARD SHAW

Jew, Turk or atheist
May enter here, but not a papist

Whoever wrote this wrote it well
For the same is written in the gates of Hell.

— ANONYMOUS, 17th-century rhyme written on walls of
Bandon town and the reply that appeared afterwards.

There is no wild beast so ferocious as Christians who differ concerning their faith.

—W. E. H. LECKY, *History of the Rise and Influence of the Spirit of Rationalism in Europe,* 1866

⊚⊗⊚

Religion in our town had arrayed the inhabitants into two hostile camps. She never had any sympathy with the fight.... She pointed out to the fanatics around her that the basis of religion was love and that religion that expressed itself in faction fights must have hate at the bottom of it.

—ALEXANDER IRVINE, *My Lady of the Chimney Corner,* 1915

⊚⊗⊚

In Northern Ireland, if you don't have basic Christianity, rather than merely religion, all you get out of the experience of living is bitterness.

—BERNADETTE DEVLIN, *The Price of My Soul,* 1969

⊚⊗⊚

Ireland remains a deeply religious country, with the two main denominations being "us" and "them."

—FRANK MCNALLY, *Irish Times,* March 11, 1998

Catholicism enriched my life, guided my actions, and fed my political belief in the capacity and responsibility to alleviate suffering. Catholicism was integrated into every aspect of my family's intellectual, moral, social, cultural, political, and spiritual life. It was impossible to separate the influence of the Church from that of our Irish heritage or Democratic politics.

—KERRY KENNEDY, Preface to *Being Catholic Now*
edited by Kerry Kennedy, 2008

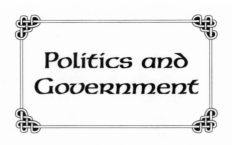

Politics and Government

Our ancestors believed in magic, prayers, trickery, brow-
beating and bullying: I think it would be fair to sum that
list up as "Irish politics."

> —FLANN O'BRIEN, *The Hair of the Dogma,* 1977

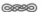

Politics is the chloroform of the Irish people, or, rather,
the hashish.

> — OLIVER ST. JOHN GOGARTY,
> *As I Was Going Down Sackville Street,* 1937

Nothing is politically right which is morally wrong.

> —DANIEL O'CONNELL, Letter to the Earl of Shrewsbury

Politics and Government

I have no political ambitions for myself or my children.

—JOSEPH P. KENNEDY, *I'm for Roosevelt,* 1936

⊗≈⊗

Mothers may still want their favorite sons to grow up to be
President, but, according to a famous Gallop poll of some years
ago, they do not want them to become politicians in the process.

—JOHN F. KENNEDY, *Profiles in Courage,* 1956

⊗≈⊗

In politics you have no friends, only allies.

—JOHN F. KENNEDY, quoted in *Honey Fitz: Three Steps to the
White House* by John Henry Cutler, 1962

⊗≈⊗

I lost the first race I ever ran, for the Cambridge City Council,
by 160 votes because I took my own neighborhood for granted.
My father took me aside after the election and told me, "All
politics is local. Don't forget it."

—TIP O'NEILL, *All Politics Is Local,*
Tip O'Neill with Gary Hymel, 1994

The politician . . . is the philosopher in action.

—EDMUND BURKE, *Thoughts on the Cause of the Present Discontents*, April 23, 1770

Much has been made of the way the women's vote went to her. I suspect that what was so evident as to draw comment was the proud jubilance of women voters at having a splendid candidate to vote for who also happened, icing-on-a-cake fashion, to be a woman. That was one in the eye for the ah-ya-boy-ya crowd, all right. But what's truly significant is that she got the men's vote . . . the men of Ireland went unhesitatingly out and voted for a woman president because she represented their views.

—MARY MAHER, on the election of Mary Robinson, *Irish Times*, November 12, 1990

Look at the Lord's disciples. One denied Him, one doubted Him, one betrayed Him. If our Lord couldn't have perfection, how are you going to have it in city government?

—RICHARD J. DALEY, quoted in *Through Irish Eyes*, edited by Tracy Quinn, 1999

The single most exciting thing you can encounter in government is competence, because it is so rare.

—DANIEL PATRICK MOYNIHAN

A government which robs Peter to pay Paul can always depend on the support of Paul.

— GEORGE BERNARD SHAW,
Everybody's Political What's What?, 1944

Democracy means simply the bludgeoning of the people by the people for the people.

— OSCAR WILDE, "The Soul of Man Under Socialism,"
Fortnightly Review, February 1891

The Massachusetts ticket is all Irish; its members have the cold eyes and slack faces of IRA members who have gone into another line of work.

—MURRAY KEMPTON, *America Comes of Middle Age*, 1968

All the ills of democracy can be cured by more democracy.

—ALFRED E. SMITH

⊚⊗⊛⊚

The majority of the members of the Irish parliament are professional politicians, in the sense that otherwise they would not be given jobs minding mice at crossroads.

—FLANN O'BRIEN, *The Hair of the Dogma,* 1977

⊚⊗⊛⊚

He knows nothing; and he thinks he knows everything. That points clearly to a political career.

— GEORGE BERNARD SHAW, *Major Barbara,* 1905

⊚⊗⊛⊚

The only people who will be able to get to Congress will be the half-witted sons of the rich. The bright sons of the rich are needed to run the businesses, and the poor cannot afford to run.

—TIP O'NEILL

In our brief national history we have shot four of our presidents, worried five of them to death, impeached one, and hounded another out of office. And when all else fails, we hold an election and assassinate their character.

—P. J. O'ROURKE, *Parliament of Whores*, 1991

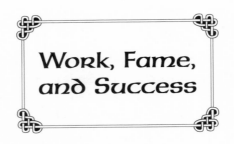

Work, Fame, and Success

Irish Americans, like other American ethnics, built occupational networks too. Burrowing into specific trades or industries they created "niches" for their own people. New York City's fire department, with its hive of Irish-American friends and relatives, is a classic example of this kind of niche, but there have been others. In New York, Irish Americans also established substantial niches among the longshoremen and transit workers at one time or another, and dominated the city's police department for decades.

—"The Fireman on the Stairs: Communal Loyalties in the Making of Irish America" by Timothy J. Meagher in *Radharc: A Journal of Irish Studies, Volume 4,* 2003

For just experience tells, in every soil, that those that think must govern those that toil.

— OLIVER GOLDSMITH, "The Traveller," 1764

Work, Fame, and Success

We worked on the subways, we ran the saloons
We built all the bridges, we played all the tunes
We put out the fires and controlled City Hall
We started with nothing and wound up with it all.

—TERENCE WINCH, "When New York Was Irish,"
Songs and Tunes by Terence Winch, 2007

People are always blaming their circumstances for what they
are. I don't believe in circumstances. The people who get
on in this world are the people who get up and look for the
circumstances they want, and, if they can't find them, make
them.

— GEORGE BERNARD SHAW, *Mrs. Warren's Profession,* 1893

I'm a firm believer in the theory that people only do their best
at things they truly enjoy.

—JACK NICKLAUS

All progress is based upon a universal innate desire on the part of every organism to live beyond its income.

—SAMUEL BUTLER, *The Note-Books of Samuel Butler*
edited by Henry Festing Jones, 1907

The artist, like the God of creation, remains within or behind or beyond or above his handiwork, invisible, refined out of existence, indifferent, paring his fingernails.

—JAMES JOYCE, *A Portrait of the Artist as a Young Man,* 1916

Painting became everything to me ... Through it I made articulate all that I saw and felt, all that went on inside the mind that was housed within my useless body like a prisoner in a cell.

—CHRISTY BROWN, *My Left Foot,* 1954

Of all human struggles there is none so treacherous and remorseless as the struggle between the artist man and the mother woman.

—GEORGE BERNARD SHAW, *Man and Superman,* 1903

Conditions in the industry somehow propose the paradox: "We brought you here for your individuality but while you're here we insist that you do everything to conceal it."

—F. SCOTT FITZGERALD, writing about the movie industry, *The Letters of F. Scott Fitzgerald* edited by Andrew Turnbull, 1963

I have never liked working. To me a job is an invasion of privacy.

—DANNY MCGOORTY

A perpetual holiday is a good working definition of Hell.

—GEORGE BERNARD SHAW, "The Horror of the Perpetual Holiday," *Parents and Children,* 1914

The highest price you have to pay for becoming a celebrity is that you become a fugitive.

—CARROLL O'CONNOR, *Playboy,* January 1973

You can't shame or humiliate modern celebrities. What used to be called shame and humiliation is now called publicity.

—P. J. O'ROURKE, *Give War a Chance,* 1992

When a young man came up to him in Zurich and said, "May I kiss the hand that wrote *Ulysses?*" Joyce replied, somewhat like King Lear, "No, it did lots of other things too."

—JAMES JOYCE, quoted in *James Joyce* by Richard Ellmann, 1959

Once I went over to the House Democratic Club for lunch and I found myself in the "O'Neill Room," very kindly dedicated in my honor. I was even standing under a portrait of my Irish self. The maitre d' looked up and said, "Do you have a reservation?" How quickly they forget.

—TIP O'NEILL, *All Politics Is Local,* by Tip O'Neill with Gary Hymel, 1994

Music is spiritual. The music business is not.

—VAN MORRISON, *The Times,* July 6, 1990

If my books had been any worse I should not have been invited to Hollywood, and if they had been any better I should not have come.

—RAYMOND CHANDLER, letter to Charles W. Morton,
December 12, 1945

It's easy to make a buck. It's a lot tougher to make a difference.

—TOM BROKAW

It is better to be young in your failures than old in your successes.

—FLANNERY O'CONNOR

It's how you deal with failure that determines how you achieve success.

—DAVID FEHERTY

The truth is, we are like any other oppressed race—it's impressed on us that, as subhumans, we're in bondage because our oppressors are superior to us in every way. Thus the dimmest nitwit Brit considers himself superior to the most brilliant Irisher, by birth and by virtue of force of arms. And we bought it, every ounce of it. We groveled and fawned and tugged the forelock and imitated them, because we thought that's the way to get on. Because we learned to despise ourselves, we wanted desperately to become someone else. So with all our hearts, minds, souls, brains, and spirits, we did become someone else, thus laying the foundations of a nation that has produced not good, but great, actors.

—MALACHY MCCOURT

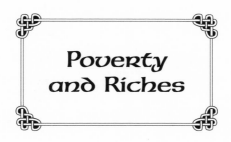

Poverty and Riches

I have seen the Indian in his forests and the negro in his irons, and I believed, in pitying their plight, that I saw the lowest ebb of human misery; but I did not then know the degree of poverty to be found in Ireland.

— GUSTAVE DE BEAUMONT, *L'Irlande sociale, politique et religieuse,* 1839

Laws grind the poor, and rich men rule the law.

— OLIVER GOLDSMITH, *The Traveller,* 1764

The real tragedy of the poor is that they can afford nothing but self-denial.

— OSCAR WILDE, *The Picture of Dorian Gray,* 1891

THE ESSENTIAL WISDOM OF THE IRISH

The greatest of evils and the worst of crimes is poverty.

—GEORGE BERNARD SHAW, preface to *Major Barbara,* 1907

Mother realised, to her great astonishment, that Betty was
a Protestant as well. Nobody had ever explained to her that
Protestants could also be poor.

—FRANK O'CONNOR, *An Only Child,* 1961

To marry the Irish is to look for poverty.

—J. P. DONLEAVY, *The Ginger Man,* 1955

There is only one class in the community that thinks more
about money than the rich, and that is the poor. The poor can
think of nothing else.

—OSCAR WILDE, "The Soul of Man Under Socialism,"
Fortnightly Review, February 1891

Lack of money is the root of all evil.

— GEORGE BERNARD SHAW

There's only one thing to do with loose change of course. Tighten it.

—FLANN O'BRIEN, *The Best of Myles*, 1968

It is better to have a permanent income than to be fascinating.

— OSCAR WILDE

People with a culture of poverty suffer much less from repression than we of the middle class suffer and indeed, if I may make the suggestion with due qualification, they often have a hell of a lot more fun than we have.

—BRIAN FRIEL, *The Freedom of the City*, 1973

Our middle classes, who are comfortable and irresponsible at other people's expense ... are neither ashamed of that condition nor even conscious of it.

— GEORGE BERNARD SHAW, preface to *St. Joan,* 1923

⸎

A wise man should have money in his head but not in his heart.

—JONATHAN SWIFT

⸎

Let me tell you about the very rich. They are different from you and me.

—F. SCOTT FITZGERALD, remark to Ernest Hemingway, who said in reply, "Yes, they have more money."

⸎

Nothing is so hard for those who abound in riches to conceive how others can be in want.

—JONATHAN SWIFT, letter to Lord Bolingbroke, April 5, 1729

⸎

Money gave me exactly what I wanted, power over others.

—OSCAR WILDE, *An Ideal Husband,* 1895

It's a good thing to be able to take up your money in your hand and to think no more of it when it slips away from you than you would of a trout that would slip back into the stream.

—LADY ISABELLA AUGUSTA GREGORY, *Twenty-Five,* 1908

The more I see of the moneyed classes, the more I understand the guillotine.

— GEORGE BERNARD SHAW, letter dated September 25, 1899

Wealth often takes away chances from men as well as poverty. There is none to tell the rich to go on striving, for a rich man makes the law that hallows and hollows his own life.

—SEAN O'CASEY, *Rose and Crown* Vol. 5,
"Pennsylvanian Visit," 1952

If a free society cannot help the many who are poor, it cannot save the few who are rich.

—JOHN F. KENNEDY, inaugural address, January 20, 1961

The surest way to ruin a man who doesn't know how to handle money is to give him some.

— GEORGE BERNARD SHAW, *Heartbreak House*, 1920

I am a Millionaire. That is my religion.

— GEORGE BERNARD SHAW, *Major Barbara*, 1907

We *can* be the generation that no longer accepts that an accident of latitude determines whether a child lives or dies. But *will* we be that generation?

—BONO, foreword to *The End of Poverty* by Jeffrey Sachs, 2005

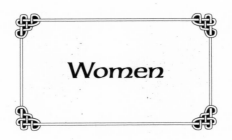

Women

What a misfortune it is to be born a woman! . . .
Why seek for knowledge, which can prove only that
our wretchedness is irremediable? If a ray of life break in upon
us, it is but to make darkness more visible; to show us the
new limits, the Gothic structure, the impenetrable barriers
of our prison.

—MARIA EDGEWORTH, *Leonara*, 1806

Women are wiser than men because they know less and
understand more.

—JAMES STEPHENS, *The Crock of Gold*, 1912

The worker is the slave of the capitalist society, the female
worker is the slave of that slave.

—JAMES CONNOLLY, *The Reconquest of Ireland*, 1915

The vote, I thought, means nothing to women. We should be armed.

—EDNA O'BRIEN

One thing she had in abundance—physical courage: with that she was clothed as with a garment.

—SEAN O'CASEY on Constance Markievicz,
Drums Under the Window

My mother didn't want anything to do with child-rearing or housework. But she had to do it. Because she fell in love with my father, and they married, she was condemned to spend her life as a mother and a homemaker. She was in the wrong job. Sometimes I meet women who remind me of her when I stay in bed-and-breakfasts around the country. They throw sugar on the fire, to get it to light, and wipe surfaces with an old rag that smells, and they are forever sending children to the shops. They question me, half censorious, half wistful: "And did you never want to get married yourself?"

—NUALA O'FAOLAIN, *Are You Somebody?*, 1996

We women adore failures. They lean on us.

> —OSCAR WILDE, *A Woman of No Importance,* 1893

All women become like their mothers. That is their tragedy.
No man does. That's his.

> —OSCAR WILDE, *The Importance of Being Ernest,* 1895

I think being a woman is like being Irish. . . . Everyone says
you're important and nice, but you take second place all
the same.

> —IRIS MURDOCH, *The Red and the Green,* 1965

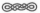

If you want to push something in politics, you're accused of
being aggressive, and that's not supposed to be a good thing
for a woman. If you get upset and show it, you're accused of
being emotional.

> —MARY HARNEY

I was elected by the women of Ireland, who instead of rocking the cradle, rocked the system.

—MARY ROBINSON, in her victory speech as president,
quoted in *The Times*, November 10, 1990

All her life she was to personify the best of her Irish heritage—a warm and generous heart, undauntable faith in her God, unswerving allegiance to the Democratic Party, heroic resiliency in trouble and always, always, and unquenchable sense of humor.

—MARY HIGGINS CLARK, "My Wild Irish Mother," 1977

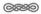

My grandmother always said that one life lived well can make a difference, and I think it is up to all women to have faith in the value and integrity of their own contribution to the world they live in.

—MARY MCALEESE, interview in *Kennedy School Bulletin,* 1999

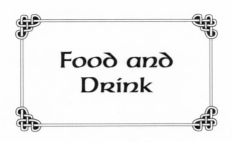

Food and Drink

Intemperate eating kills more people than tobacco and alcohol, because it is the most widespread fault.... If people knew how to eat properly they would retain their youthful resiliency much longer.

—HENRY FORD, *The Metaphysics of Henry Ford*
by George Sylvester Viereck, 1930

There is no love sincerer than the love of food.

—GEORGE BERNARD SHAW, *Man and Superman,* 1903

He was a bold man that first ate an oyster.

—JONATHAN SWIFT, *Polite Conversation*

My mother tells me she's worn out pouring tinned sauce over the frozen chicken.

—MAEVE BINCHY, *Evening Class,* 1996

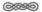

When money's tight and is hard to get
And your horse has also ran,
When all you have is a heap of debt—
A pint of plain is your only man.

—FLANN O'BRIEN, *At Swim-Two-Birds,* 1939

I only take a drink on two occasions—when I'm thirsty and when I'm not.

—BRENDAN BEHAN, *The Wit of Brendan Behan*
compiled by Sean McCann, 1968

Under the pressure of the cares and sorrows of our mortal condition, men have at all times, and in all countries, called in some physical aid to their moral consolations—wine, beer, opium, brandy, or tobacco.

—EDMUND BURKE, "Thoughts and Details on Scarcity," 1795

Food and Drink

The most important thing to remember about drunks is
that drunks are far more intelligent than non-drunks. They
spend a lot of time talking in pubs, unlike workaholics who
concentrate on their careers and ambitions, who never develop
their higher spiritual values, who never explore the insides
of their head like a drunk does.

—SHANE MACGOWAN, lead singer and songwriter for The Pogues

When I realized what I had turned out to be was a lousy,
two-bit pool hustler and a drunk, I wasn't depressed at all.
I was glad to have a profession.

—DANNY MCGOORTY, Irish pool player

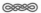

It's the first drop that destroys you, there's no harm at all in
the last.

—IRISH PROVERB

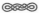

When I die I want to decompose in a barrel of porter and
have it served in all the pubs in Dublin.

—J. P. DONLEAVY

Work is the curse of the drinking classes.

—OSCAR WILDE, *Life of Oscar Wilde* by H. Pearson, 1946

∞∞∞

"Poteen" is the most mysterious word in the country places of Ireland. It is never spoken: it is always whispered. This illicit firewater, which is distilled in the dead of night, or on misty days which hide the smoke from the still, has always been made in the lonely hills of Ireland.

—H. V. MORTON, *In Search of Ireland,* 1930

∞∞∞

Alcohol is a very necessary article . . . it enables Parliament to do things at eleven at night that no sane person would do at eleven in the morning.

—GEORGE BERNARD SHAW, *Major Barbara,* 1907

∞∞∞

When you stop drinking, you have to deal with this marvelous personality that started you drinking in the first place.

—JIMMY BRESLIN

Food and Drink

One drink is too many for me and a thousand not enough.

—BRENDAN BEHAN

May your glass be ever full, May the roof over your head be
 always strong,
And may you be in Heaven
Half an hour before the devil knows you're dead.

—IRISH TOAST

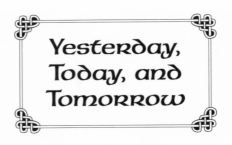

Yesterday, Today, and Tomorrow

We Irish are always being accused of looking backwards too much. Sometimes, however, we don't look back far enough—or carefully enough, or honestly enough.

—DERVLA MURPHY, *A Place Apart,* 1978

Men have been dying for Ireland since the beginning of time and look at the state of the country.

—FRANK MCCOURT, *Angela's Ashes,* 1996

History, Stephen said, is a nightmare from which I am trying to awake.

—JAMES JOYCE, *Ulysses,* 1922

Hegel was right when he said that we learn from history that we learn nothing from history.

— GEORGE BERNARD SHAW, Preface to *Heartbreak House,* 1920

Anybody can make history. Only a great man can write it.

— OSCAR WILDE, "The Critic as Artist," 1890

Few will have the greatness to bend history itself; but each of us can work to change a small portion of events, and in the total of all those acts will be written the history of this generation.

—ROBERT F. KENNEDY, Day of Affirmation address, University of Capetown, South Africa, June 1966

It's not perfect, but to me on balance Right Now is a lot better than the Good Old Days.

—MAEVE BINCHY, *Irish Times,* November 15, 1997

The day of the dinosaurs is over. The future belongs to the bridge-builders, not the wreckers.

—MARY MCALEESE, on the election to the Northern Irish Assembly, *Irish Times*, June 27, 1998

I want to see an Ireland of partnership where we wage war on want and poverty, where we reach out to the marginalized and dispossessed, where we build together a future that can be as great as our dreams allow.

—JOHN HUME, Nobel Peace Prize acceptance speech, 1998

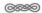

Remember the Celtic Tiger? Well, she turned out to be a pussycat with a shamrock. Ireland was the hot country of the 2000s as youth from throughout the euro zone flocked there for jobs in finance, software development, restaurants, what have you . . . That was then. A property bubble burst badly, leaving Irish banks technically insolvent and the government deeply in debt . . . the Irish government pledges to cut more, but you can't get blood from a blarney stone.

—HOWARD GOLD, Marketwatch.com, September 27, 2010

If in the future we are to avoid the extremes of economic boom and bust scenarios, we need not only smart and rigorous regulatory systems that allow commerce to flourish, where the regulator has all the powers and competences, but we need professionals who are hard-wired to behave ethically, to think ethically, to act ethically, to respect the requirement of compliance, to understand and see themselves as operating in the broad public interest.

—MARY McALEESE, quoted in the *Belfast Telegraph*, September 11, 2010

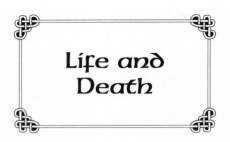

Life and Death

The master says it's a glorious thing to die for the Faith and Dad says it's a glorious thing to die for Ireland and I wonder if there's anyone in the world who would like us to live.

—FRANK MCCOURT, *Angela's Ashes,* 1996

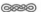

Never to have lived is best, ancient writers say;
Never to have drawn the breath of life,
Never to have looked into the eye of day;
The second best's a gay goodnight and quickly turn away.

—W. B. YEATS, *Oedipus at Colonus,* 1928

One can live for years sometimes without living at all, and then all life comes crowding into one single hour.

—OSCAR WILDE, *Vera, or The Nihilist,* 1880

Life and Death

What I shall do with this absurdity
O heart, O troubled heart—this caricature
Decrepit age that has been tied to me
As to a dog's tail.

—W. B. YEATS, "The Tower," 1928

Misfortunes one can endure—they come from outside, they are accidents. But to suffer for one's own faults—ah!—there is the sting of life.

— OSCAR WILDE, *Lady Windermere's Fan,* 1892

Every man desires to live long, but no man would be old.

—JONATHAN SWIFT, "Thoughts on Various Subjects,"
Miscellanies in Prose and Verse, Vol. 1, 1727

What is the life of man? Is it not to shift from side to side, from sorrow to sorrow?—to button up one cause of vexation and unbutton another.

—LAURENCE STERNE, *Tristram Shandy,* 1759–1767

The old—like children—talk to themselves, for they have reached that hopeless wisdom of experience which knows that though one were to cry it in the streets to multitudes, or whisper it in the kiss to one's beloved, the only ears that can ever hear one's secrets are one's own!

—EUGENE O'NEILL, *Lazarus Laughed,* 1925

When you are old and gray and full of sleep,
And nodding by the fire, take down this book,
And slowly read, and dream of the soft look
Your eyes had once, and of their shadows deep;

How many loved your moments of glad grace,
And loved your beauty with love false or true,
But one man loved the pilgrim soul in you
And loved the sorrows of your changing face;

And bending down beside the glowing bars
Murmur, a little sadly, how love fled
And paced upon the mountains overhead
And hid his face amid a crowd of stars.

—W. B. YEATS, "When You Are Old," *The Rose,* 1893

To get back my youth I would do anything in the world, except take exercise, get up early, or be respectable.

— OSCAR WILDE, *The Picture of Dorian Gray,* 1891

❦

Life does not cease to be funny when people die any more than it ceases to be serious when people laugh.

— GEORGE BERNARD SHAW, *The Doctor's Dilemma,* 1906

❦

It often happens that the real tragedies of life occur in such an inartistic manner that they hurt us by their crude violence, their absolute incoherence, their absurd want of meaning, their entire lack of style.

— OSCAR WILDE, *The Picture of Dorian Gray,* 1891

❦

A life spent in making mistakes is not only more honorable but more useful than a life spent doing nothing.

— GEORGE BERNARD SHAW, "Preface on Doctors," *The Doctor's Dilemma,* 1906

I've put in so many enigmas and puzzles that it will keep the professors busy for centuries arguing over what I meant, and that's the only way of insuring one's immortality.

—JAMES JOYCE, commenting on *Ulysses*

Dying is a troublesome business: there is pain to be suffered, and it wrings one's heart; but death is a splendid thing—a warfare accomplished, a beginning all over again, a triumph. You can always see that in their faces.

— GEORGE BERNARD SHAW, letter of condolence, July 1913

I want to be thoroughly used up when I die, for the harder I work the more I live. I rejoice in life for its own sake. Life is no "brief candle" for me. It is a sort of splendid torch which I have got hold of for the moment, and I want to make it burn as brightly as possible before handing it on to future generations.

— GEORGE BERNARD SHAW

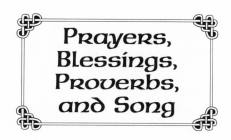

Prayers, Blessings, Proverbs, and Song

Christ with me, Christ before me, Christ behind me,
Christ in me, Christ beneath me, Christ above me,
Christ on my right, Christ on my left,
Christ when I lie down, Christ when I sit down, Christ when
    I arise.
Christ in the heart of every man who thinks of me,
Christ in the mouth of every one who speaks of me,
Christ in every eye that sees me,
Christ in every ear that hears me.

—ANONYMOUS, from St. Patrick's breastplate, 8th century.
Translated from the Irish by Kuno Meyer

Up the airy mountain,
Down the rushy glen,
We daren't go a-hunting,
For fear of little men.

—WILLIAM ALLINGHAM, "The Fairies," 1850

You've blessed me with friends
and laughter and fun
With rain that's as soft
as the light from the sun—
You've blessed me with stars
to brighten each night
You've given me help
to know wrong from right—
You've given me so much
please, Lord give me too,
A heart that is always
Grateful to you.

—An Irish prayer

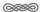

May the road rise to meet you.
May the wind be always at your back.
May the sun shine warm upon your face;
The rains fall soft upon your fields
And, until we meet again,
May God hold you in the palm of His hand.

—A Gaelic blessing

There's a dear little plant that grows in Ireland.
'Twas Saint Patrick himself sure that set it.
And the sun on his labour with pleasure did smile.
And a tear from his eyes oft-times wet it.
It grows thro' the bog, thro' the brake, and the mireland,
And it's called the dear little Shamrock of Ireland.

—ANDREW CHERRY, "The Dear Little Shamrock"

Have you ever been in love, me boys
Oh! have you felt the pain,
I'd rather be in gaol, I would,
Than be in love again.

—JOHNNY PATTERSON, "The Garden Where the Praties Grow,"
19th-century ballad

Come all you young rebels and list while I sing
For the love of one's land is a terrible thing
It banishes fear with the speed of a flame
And makes us all part of the patriot game.

—DOMINIC BEHAN, "The Patriot Game," 1959

May you be poor in misfortune, rich in blessings, slow to make enemies and quick to make friends. And may you know nothing but happiness from this day forward.

—WEDDING TOAST

Oh, Danny boy, the pipes, the pipes are calling,
From glen to glen and down the mountainside,
The summer's gone and all the roses falling,
'Tis you, 'tis you must go and I must bide,
But come ye back when summer's in the meadow,
Or when the valley's hushed and white with snow.
'Tis I'll be there in sunshine or in shadow,
Oh Danny boy, Oh Danny boy I love you so.

And when you come and all the flowers are dying,
If I am dead—and dead I well may be,
Ye'll come and find a place where I am lying,
And kneel and say an *Ave* there for me;
And I shall hear though soft your tread above me,
And all my grave shall warmer, sweeter be,
For you will bend and tell me that you love me,
And I shall sleep in peace until you come to me.

—Written by FRED WEATHERLY, early 20th century, sung to
the tune of the ancient Irish melody, "The Derry Air,"
quoted in *Touch of the Irish* edited by Sean Desmond

The three most beautiful sights: a potato garden in bloom, a ship in sail, a woman after the birth of her child.

∞∞∞

Be kind to those you meet as you rise, you may pass them again as you fall.

∞∞∞

There are as many good fish in the sea as ever came out of it.

∞∞∞

If you get a reputation as an early riser, you can sleep till noon.

∞∞∞

The horse that earns the oats never gets them.

∞∞∞

The best looking glass is the eyes of a friend.

∞∞∞

There is not a tree in Heaven that is higher than the tree of patience.

Get down on your knees and thank God you are on your feet.

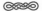

The Irish—Be they kings, or poets, or farmers, They're a
people of great worth, They keep company with the angels,
And bring a bit of Heaven here to earth.

—UNKNOWN

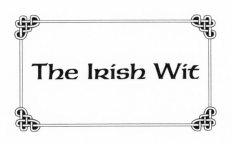

The Irish Wit

ady Carteret, wife of the Lord Lieutenant of Ireland,
praising Ireland, said to Jonathan Swift, 'Sir, the air of
your country is healthy and very excellent.' He replied, 'For
God's sake, madam, don't say so in England; for if you do they
will certainly tax it.'

—JONATHAN SWIFT, quoted in *Irish Wit*,
edited by Sean McCann, 2009

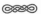

My favorite optimist was an American who jumped off the
Empire State Building, and as he passed the forty-second floor,
the window washers heard him say, "So Far, so good."

—JOHN MCGAHERN

I have nothing to declare except my genius.

—OSCAR WILDE, upon his arrival at New York Customs Hall

Blunders in speech used to be called "Irish Bulls." A lady seated beside the Provost of Dublin University said, "Dr. Mahaffy, would you tell me what is the difference between an Irish bull and another bull?" "Madam," said Dr. Mahaffy, "an Irish bull is pregnant."

—*A Treasury of Irish Folklore* edited by Padraic Colum, 1983

It used to occur to me when I lived in London . . . that it can't be easy being a queen. The poor old dear has had one *annus horribilis* after another. The kids are splitting up, the palace is falling down, the mother is on the gin. It is all like a particularly atrocious episode of *Eastenders*.

—JOSEPH O'CONNOR, *The Secret World of the Irish Male,* 1995

A charitable lady from Dublin was calling on houses in the streets of Dalkey. "I am collecting for the new home for drunkards," she said to the woman who answered the door. "Right you are," said the mistress of the house. "Come back half an hour after closing time and you can have him."

—*Touch of the Irish,* edited by Sean Desmond, 1995

When I told the people of Northern Ireland that I was an atheist, a woman in the audience stood up and said, "Yes, but is it the God of the Catholics or the God of the Protestants in whom you don't believe?"

— QUENTIN CRISP

An Irish atheist is one who wishes to God he could believe in God.

—JOHN PENTLAND MAHAFFY

Irish Alzheimer's: you forget everything except the grudges.

—JUDY COLLINS

I was a loner as a child. I had an imaginary friend—I didn't bother with him.

— GEORGE CARLIN

I've always admired the American constitution. I mean, to be able to stuff so much food into their faces in such a short time requires an incredible constitution.

—SINEAD MURPHY

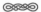

Laughter is wine for the soul—laughter soft, or loud and deep, tinged through with seriousness—the hilarious declaration made by man that life is worth living.

—SEAN O'CASEY

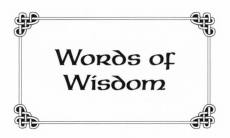

Words of Wisdom

Those who are animated by hope can perform what would seem impossibilities to those who are under the depressing influence of fear.

—Maria Edgeworth, "The Grateful Negro," 1804

Life is not meant to be easy, my child; but take courage: it can be delightful.

—George Bernard Shaw, *Back to Methusela,* 1921

I sometimes suspect that half our difficulties are imaginary and that if we kept quiet about them they would disappear.

—Robert Lynd

There are two tragedies in life. One is not to get your heart's desire. The other is to get it.

— GEORGE BERNARD SHAW, *Man and Superman*, 1903

⚭

The great secret . . . is not having bad manners or good manners or any other particular sort of manners, but having the same manner for all human souls: in short, behaving as if you were in Heaven, where there are no third-class carriages, and one soul is as good as another.

— GEORGE BERNARD SHAW, *Pygmalion*, 1912

⚭

Some cause happiness wherever they go; others whenever they go.

— OSCAR WILDE

⚭

It is useless to hold a person to anything he says while he is in love, drunk, or running for office.

— SHIRLEY MACLAINE

In a conversation, keep in mind that you're more interested in what you have to say than anyone else is.

—ANDY ROONEY, *Pieces of My Mind,* 1987

One of the very best rules in conversation is, never to say a thing which any of the company can reasonably wish we had rather left unsaid.

—JONATHAN SWIFT, "Hints Toward an Essay on Conversation"

Education is an admirable thing, but it is well to remember from time to time that nothing that is worth knowing can be taught.

—OSCAR WILDE, "The Critic as Artist," 1890

When a true genius appears in the world you may know him by this sign: that all the dunces are in confederacy against him.

—JONATHAN SWIFT, "Thoughts on Various Subjects, Moral and Diverting," 1706

Education is not filling a bucket, but lighting a fire.

—W. B. YEATS

A man of genius makes no mistakes. His errors are volitional and are the portals of discovery.

—JAMES JOYCE, *Ulysses*, 1922

You see things; and you say "Why?" But I dream things that never were; and I say "Why not?"

—GEORGE BERNARD SHAW, *Back to Methuselah*, 1921

Do the best you can in every task, no matter how unimportant it may seem at the time. No one learns more about a problem than the person at the bottom.

—SANDRA DAY O'CONNOR

Ever tried. Ever failed. No matter. Try again. Fail again. Fail better.

—SAMUEL BECKETT, *Worstward Ho,* 1983

There is hope for all of us. Well, anyway, if you don't die you live through it, day in, day out.

—MARY BECKETT, *A Belfast Woman,* 1987

Chronology
of Irish History

432. St. Patrick arrives in Ireland and the process of conversion to Christianity begins. Introduction of written history.

800. Ireland is attacked by Viking Norsemen. The raids continue for two centuries.

999. Brian Boru, born in 940, defeats the Vikings.

1002. Brian Boru becomes High King of Ireland.

1014. King Boru is killed at the battle of Clontarf, where the Irish defeat the Vikings.

1066. Normans defeat the Saxons in England.

1166. Rory O'Connor reigns as the last native High King of Ireland.

1167–1169. Normans arrive in Ireland, igniting the 800-year struggle between the English and the Irish.

1169–1171. Anglo-Norman Conquest gives England sovereignty of Ireland until the creation of the Irish Free State in 1922.

1366. Statute of Kilkenny forbids marriage between the Irish and the English, and prevents the use of Irish language, custom, or laws.

1534. Henry VIII breaks with the Roman Catholic Church; failed Kildare Rebellion. Ireland is ruled by the senior nobles and English monarchy. In 1541, in an attempt to tighten his control over Ireland, Henry declares himself King of Ireland. The Irish parliament assents.

1556. Queen Mary sends Protestant English and Scottish settlers to the land taken from Irish rebels in order to increase British control over the colony.

1558. Accession of Elizabeth I.

1562. The beginning of the Elizabethan Wars in Ireland.

1593–1603. Nine Years War. Rebellion led by Hugh O'Neill, who was eventually defeated at the Battle of Kinsale (1601). James I gains the throne, and the enforcement of English law in Ireland is maintained. O'Neill and others took part in the Flight of the Earls (1607) whereby many from the old Irish nobility fled Ireland believing their plans for future rebellion had been betrayed. The earls remained exiled in Rome until their deaths, while their land in Ulster was confiscated.

1641–1649. English Civil War and Irish rebellion for the return of lands. The Irish in Ulster rise up and kill some Protestant settlers. In 1649, Oliver Cromwell arrived in Dublin and killed 2,000 men, and the majority of Irish lands were taken and divided among the English. By Cromwell's death in 1658, the Irish population was reduced by two-thirds, due in part to 60,000 Irish Catholics sent as slaves to work in the Caribbean.

1650. Catholic landowners are exiled to Connaught (westerly province). Lands are redistributed to those who have given service, known as "planters."

1660. Accession of Charles II.

1685. Accession of James II.

1689. Siege of Derry. James II restores land confiscated since 1641.

1690. William of Orange defeats James II at Battle of the Boyne and escapes to France. William's victory is an important symbolic Protestant victory that is celebrated annually.

1691. At the Battle of Aughrim, the army of James II is defeated and surrenders at Limerick.

1695. Anti-Catholic Penal Laws are introduced: laws aimed to restrict Catholic worship, participation in politics, access to education, right to bear arms, and to prohibit landownership.

1740. Approximately 400,000 die in what is now called The Forgotten Famine.

1798. The Rebellion of 1798, considered one of the most violent events in Irish history, erupts, claiming some thirty thousand lives. Society of United Irishmen organized the uprising seeking radical parliamentary reform and total Catholic emancipation. In the decisive battle of Vinegar Hill, the rebels were routed. Rebel leader Wolfe Tone commits suicide.

1801. Act of Union: Ireland becomes part of the United Kingdom. The Irish Parliament is dissolved.

1803. Robert Emmet's rebellion is crushed and Emmet is executed.

1823. Daniel O'Connell Catholic Association is founded, aimed at achieving full Catholic emancipation through legal means. About 400,000 Catholics became members.

1829. Catholic Emancipation Act is passed, giving Catholics the right to sit in Parliament. A series of relief acts in the latter 1700s had repealed many of the restrictions of the Penal Laws and restored the rights of Catholics to acquire property and the right to vote in elections.

1837. Accession of Queen Victoria.

1845–1849. The Irish Potato Famine. Immediate cause of Famine is blight on potato crop that strikes three out of four years. Population drops from 8.5 million to 6.5 million as a result of the Famine-related death and emigration.

1858. James Stephens founds Irish Republican Brotherhood. A rising in March of 1867 is quickly put down, but the campaign for amnesty to the "Fenian" (members of the Irish nationalist secret society) prisoners and sympathy for the execution of three Fenians in Manchester ("Manchester Martyrs") garners widespread public support and fuels the home rule movement.

1869. Prime Minister Gladstone disestablishes the Protestant Church of Ireland.

1875. Charles Stewart Parnell elected MP (Member of Parliament) for County Meath.

1880. Parnell becomes Irish Parliamentary Party leader and leader of the Land League aimed at bringing about land reform.

1886. Gladstone's Home Rule Bill is rejected by British parliament. Successive bills are introduced in 1893 and 1912.

1914. Outbreak of World War I.

1916. Easter Rising in Dublin occurs on April 24. Three thousand are injured and 450 killed in the uprising. The execution of the rebel leaders makes them into martyrs and inspires tremendous support for the cause of a free Ireland.

1919. Irish War of Independence against Britain ends in the Anglo-Irish Treaty.

1921. Under the Treaty, twenty-six counties of Ireland became the Irish Free State with the six counties of the north having an option to opt out of the Irish Free State.

1922. Irish Civil War between the Free State Army and the Irish Republican Army (IRA), a faction determined to see all of Ireland free from British rule. Free State leader Michael Collins is killed.

1923. End of Civil War.

1926. Revolutionary leader Eamon De Valera founds Fianna Fáil, a new political party.

1932–1937. De Valera serves as Prime Minister.

1937. The Constitution of Ireland is enacted.

1939–1945. World War II. Ireland remains neutral.

1948. J. A. Costello becomes Taoiseach, Prime Minister, in the new Dáil.

1949. Republic of Ireland declared. The Ireland Act, reaffirming the status of Northern Ireland as part of the United Kingdom is passed by the House of Commons.

1951. After a general election, Fianna Fáil becomes largest party in the Dáil and de Valera becomes Taoiseach.

1951–1962. IRA campaign in North.

1969. British troops sent to Derry.

1972. Bloody Sunday (January 30). Thirteen civilians are shot by British paratroopers during civil rights march. More than 3,000 people would lose their lives during the course of the Troubles.

1973. Ireland joins the European Union (EU).

1985. Anglo-Irish Agreement between the Republic of Ireland and Britain is signed as a means of ending the Troubles.

1994. IRA declares cease-fire.

1998. The Good Friday Agreement is accepted by all parties.

1997–2007. Ireland enters a period of economic prosperity known as the Celtic Tiger years.

2008–2011. Ireland suffers a financial crisis. Country falls into recession for first time since 1980s with a sharp rise in unemployment. IMF and EU intervene with emergency bail-out package. In November 2010, Irish government publishes four-year National Recovery Plan.